silent grace

a celebration

by Sor'a Garrett
with the photo art of
Daniel Franks

Published by SHINE Publishing,
and imprint of Inspired Connections, LLC

978-0-9969037-1-4

You planted

a pregnant seed in my chest,

ready to sprout an ocean.

Crack it open, beloved.

silent grace

Dedication

There comes a time in every life where the
longing to do something and the doing of it
merge into a tangible completion. This is
one of those times. I've been writing poetry
for as long as I can remember, and I love
sharing the words that flow in this most
simple of written forms.

I created this collection of my favorite
poems as a celebration of the woman I
am becoming. This year marks my 55th
birthday, and I'm grateful for the love that
continues to blossom through me. I believe
my poems give voice to this love and to
something even more.

Most of the poems and reflections in this
book were written as a direct result of one
of many experiences with my beloved
Teacher, Elle Collier Re (Annam). Through
these experiences, I have come to know
God as something more than a concept.
I am also coming to know myself as more
than a form. More each year, I am meeting
my Self as real, everlasting, joyous Love.

Like many, I often experience divinity most vividly through nature, so many of my written inspirations begin there. I'm honored to share these words, which I know are God's way of speaking through me. Many of the poems included in this book still bring me to my knees in admiration of what called them into being.

It is my hope that these writings will offer inspiration, a glimpse of how life has lived through me, and a taste of the magnificence I see in this world.

Thank you for allowing these reflections to enter your mind and open your heart. I dedicate this book of poems to each of you, and to the silent grace that flows unending, connecting us to the Source where we are all One.

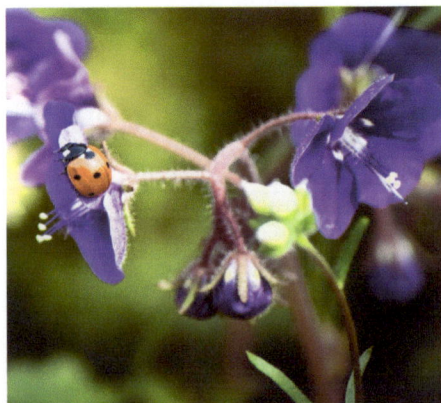

Thank You

…to my friend, Dan Franks, who generously
shares his stunning photos to add an even
greater dimension of silent grace to these
words. All of the photos in this book are his,
except where otherwise noted. Dan lives
near San Diego with my radiant friend and
creative-partner, Vasi Huntalas. More than
a partner, friend, co-creator, I have grown to
cherish Vasi as one of the best parts of my
expansive Self.

…to Jennifer Andrews, a cherished friend
who guided the final design with her creative
and graphic layup expertise, as well as a fine
eye to detail.

…and to Annam, for being a Flame of
Love so bright, so utterly devoted to God,
so generously offered to this life. Words are
never enough.

Sor'a

Contents

a celebration

How does one describe

the kind of beauty

that pours

into every cell

as eyes melt

with the simple act

of seeing?

Nature & Opening to God

Silent Grace

The daisies bow
to their Mother, drinking
in the sweet taste
of her, wet
from Heaven's rains.

I stand
in humble awe
as this picture paints before me—
how does one describe
the kind of beauty

that pours
into every cell
as eyes melt
with the simple act
of seeing?

The daisies know
that words
are not enough—
they bend
in Silent Grace;

and I bow, too,
my eyes
liquid rain, my heart
a fiery kiss
of sun

as mind at last
surrenders,
flattened
into the arms
of the Beloved.

Reflection

Silent Grace is one of my favorite poems, and I can still vividly recall the most amazing rainbow thunderstorm I've ever experienced. It called me out into the backyard, and when I saw the new spring daisies bowing beneath the wet drops of rain, I could not help but kneel beside them.

As the sun gave the earth her brilliant rays of light, the drops continued to fall lightly around me, and my heart wept with devotion and amazement. Tears poured forth from my eyes as my heart overflowed.

Then, in one single awe-ha of beautiful surrender, my mind released, simply and silently knowing God in every petal, every drop of rain, every clap of thunder.

Let this moment, and the next, and the next, drink you in. Silent grace is everywhere.

My soul knows,

and leads me exactly

where I'm meant to be.

Yours will, too.

Belief

I may never have believed anything
as much as I believe in this…
right now.

If I thought it would help, I'd shout
my heart's knowing
from the highest roof-tops.

I'd be like the blast of thunder
that shakes the ground I stand upon
at the same time it opens me in awe.

Or perhaps like the torrent
of raindrops that is giving birth
to whole new rivers
of nourishment
for this thirsty earth.

But for now I simply write this poem
and cast my vote to the wet-wild world
that blossoms all around me

planting this small seed of awareness
into the soil of Faith
that lives inside.

My soul knows, and leads me
exactly where I'm meet to be.
Yours will, too.

Listen then. Sometimes
it's just a whisper
rather than a bolt of thunder.

You're here.
All you must do now
is believe.

Reflection

This poem speaks to Faith, and to something more. The whisper, the bolt of thunder, the knowing...the quest to follow what belongs to nobody but us. This kind of belief is as essential as the air we breathe. It's what calls us awake, what brings our world more alive through the seed of passion rooted in every heart. It is, indeed, the 'Yes' that calls us into our true magnificence.

For a while I thought I had lost this Yes... the passion that has flowed through me into various projects and creations for most of my life. But I am realizing that the belief is just taking on a new form.

Rather than turning me toward a cause, or a major accomplishment, it is erupting inside my heart as a deep, quiet, everlasting, always-present faith in the present moment.

This kind of belief isn't inactive; in fact most times I am more engaged in *doing* than I have been for some time.

However, I am practicing allowing the
actions I take to arise from God's
Inspiration rather than from what
my mind creates.

I'm learning to listen more deeply than I
ever have, and to trust that what I hear will
guide me exactly where I am meant to be.

I'm here, and every day, I vow to keep
believing, and to give as fully as I can to
whatever rises before me.

Have you ever listened to a sunrise?

The music begins softly—
a whispering breeze, birdsong,
the sound of crickets, their
hind legs rubbing in glorious
celebration of a dawning day.

The melody builds. Colors paint
upon an empty slate of sky,
and if you listen closely
you will hear
the world come alive.

Flames of orange-red-yellow burst
into an awakening sky, as flames
of joy ignite my heart
with a song that sings me
into another day of being.

Whispers of cloud float lazily
across the emerging sky,
a harmonic transition
to this newborn song…and then

in one glorious moment
the symphony completes, and I
am once again unmade,
newly in love with the world
as the color of silence caresses
my mind, my heart, my eyes.

My spirit rises, bows
before this rising sun
as the music of God
sings silently
through.

If you listen closely

you will hear

the world come alive.

silent grace

20

Silent Burning

A flood
of sensations
wash my mind, yet
still the words
resist; perhaps

there *are* no words
for this symphony
of pulsing Light
that plays
through me.

Sweet melody
these senses bring, and yet
the song of my heart
is a silent
burning.

Filled with sensation
beyond words, beyond image
yet embracing
of every sense imaginable.

I begin again

each morning, my heart

an open vessel.

silent grace

Deep Well

Breathe me UP
into this great well
of God; I fell asleep
again, and come
to be renewed.

It's never enough,
this existence
of earthly domain,
no matter how clean
the essence flows through.

I begin again
each morning, my heart
an open vessel, and still
distractions weave
into my mind, this body
growing heavy with
separation.

So, every day, I ask this:
return me to the Well,

Drink me in
that I might remember
my Holy name.

Breathe me up, Beloved,
into your spring
of Eternal Love. Pour
through me, as I overflow
a bit more graciously

each time I come
to take a drink.

Reflection

Every day, the journey begins again. Every breath brings a new opportunity to open more, to forgive the body for its habit of separation. Each moment becomes a choice to give more, to love more, to wake up.

I've always had a sensitive body. From the time I was born, my mother tells me, it responded to loud noises more than her other babies. I didn't understand and tried to change it, tried to ignore the sensitivities. *(It didn't really work.)*

This being a vessel for God is intricate. The body needs support, indeed, yet if we focus too much on the body, it can become just another form of separation and isolation.

Deep Well reminds me to drink often from the pure Source, to dip into the always present ocean of God. The soul needs this nourishment as much as the body needs water; without it, our hearts dry up and die, even before the body leaves this earth.

The next poem, Vessel, is one of my all-time favorites. It also speaks of drinking from this deep well of God. It is a reflection of how we nourish one another by loving, unconditionally and without holding anything back.

I wrote this poem for my teacher, after an experience of profoundly feeling God's Love pouring through her and into my heart more completely than I ever had before. It truly did feel as if my body disappeared and we became One Vessel, pouring endlessly into the other.

We are each capable of being this for one another. As we open to receive from Source, we cannot help but allow this endless stream of giving to pour through. It isn't always easy, but the more I open my heart to drink from this holiness, the more this Great Love overflows to every One I meet.

I dedicate *Vessel* to the overflowing.

Here I am again,
thick with God

and you the vessel
from which I come to drink.

Vessel

Here I am again, thick with God,
and you the vessel
from which I come to drink—
great carafe of Love
pouring endlessly
into every open cup you find.

At first I hold my cup so close, afraid
of liquid fire,
but slowly I open a space inside,
allow you to pour deeply
my cup g r o w i n g ... g r o w i n g
and you there pouring, just pouring
so beautifully.

Then one day
my cup begins to overflow,
this fiery liquid river of Light
s t r e a m i n g
back into the world; my cup
finally disappearing,

this Great Love
pouring
right back
into You.

My cup overflows...

disappears...

this Great Love

now pours

into You.

A Good Washing

All of a sudden, the drops come—
plump, juicy morsels of wetness
f a l l i n g from Heaven
to wash me clean, awaken me
in child-like innocence
to embrace this
unexpectedly
wet moment.

Before long the clothes
are clinging to my body,
a bit like that part of you,
bravely offered,
that still clings to my heart.

My skin drinks
the moist succulence.
My heart, too:
how often it thirsts
for a deep drink
of authentic being!

Back inside now, safe behind
my window,
I watch in amazement
as drops become a river—
great currents flowing
with a steadiness that speaks to
the power of opening, fully.

A bolt of light, a clash of thunder,
and I think how we know
one another
not so much by the words offered,
but by the essence that carries them.

And I wonder how we can see
the beauty
in one another, in a thunderstorm,
but turn away from
that bright essence within.

Today, the blue sky shows
no memory
of last night's torrential rains;
but the earth remembers, as I do,
and we are both fully nourished.

Embracing the washing, I feel fresh
as this wet dirt beneath
my bare feet.

Pulsing with heart-connection,
I open
like a blossoming rose,
my Purpose strong in me.

*Now what was it
I was supposed to DO today?*

My skin drinks

the moist succulence.

My heart, too.

How often it thirsts

for a deep drink

of authentic being!

...and I wonder how we can see

the beauty in one another,

in a thunderstorm,

but turn away from

the bright essence within.

Tripping toward Heaven

If I gave you
a ladder
to the stars,
would you climb it?

If I left breadcrumbs of light
to lead you to heaven,
would you
follow them home?

This earthly existence
is filled with stumbles
& strife, with choices made
for all the wrong reasons.

The food supply of Love
is never-ending, yet it seems
our diet often consists
of only the crust.

Not that we prefer it that way,
it's just what lies before us

and we're not quite sure yet
how to dine within the Divine.

So we walk along the best we can,
tripping toward heaven,
with as much grace as
we can muster in this moment.

And meanwhile God waits,
an open invitation
to ascend heaven's ladder,
to ignite the flame…

To ignite the Flame of
an ever-awakening Heart.

Awakened Love

This, then, is love.

Not the love that
Evaporates
with each morning dew;

This love burns inside, to
Tremble
with unbridled passion.

Its pure intensity
Transforms,
explodes into Creation;

A flaming tear of
Gladness
that spreads
to an ocean of
Awakened
fire.

Just sit here now

...give your mind

to this vast Light, pouring

like a glistening waterfall

of Radiance from above.

Where the Real Play begins

Listen Now.
Your life is not your own.
You may have glimpses
of independence; and, of course,
you *do* have free will.

Otherwise, the game
would be too short, the path
a straight arrow. And where
is the fun in that?

Just sit here now; give your mind
to this vast Light, pouring
like a glistening waterfall
of Radiance from above.

Give your heart to Heaven
even as your feet
stay rooted to the earth.
You are not alone.

Come, give your life
to this Holy Flame.

Breathe it into the form
you call your body: *it is NOT you.*

Let your body be simply
a vessel for this Great Love;
Let it know itself as a reflection
of an ancient story.

Let it carry the Real You,
One step at a time
(or even in One great leap)
into the God Lane.

Now the Real Play
can begin.

The World Goes On

I don't know
what is happening tomorrow,
or who says who
is doing the wrong thing
now. I only know
the sound of this
laughing river
that moves beside me
as I sit breathing
this chill autumn air.

I only know the sparkle
of this golden sunlight
as it dances across
the musical ripples of today
as they play on my yearning heart.

My eyes see the world
differently somehow—I cannot
find despair in a sun
that rises each morning,
or trees that change color
before my humble eyes.

Do you see that tiny flower
peeking out from
beneath its emerald throne?

The world goes on
around me, a chaos
of righteous wrongs.

And who will find
the simple beauty in the
children's laughter?

Who will remember
to gaze at the starry night,
when the whole world
seems bent on finding
the next imperfect sounding
in this great symphony
called life?

Reflection

Some will call me a Pollyanna, and much
of my life I've felt too tender for this world.
The truth is, I do see, and feel, the pain that
surrounds us. I also see, appreciate, and turn
every day to the beauty that is also here.

It doesn't necessarily help ease the pain of
poverty, war, starving children…no wait.
Yes it does. Seeing the positive in life doesn't
keep my heart from breaking, but it *does*
help open my heart and encourage me to
keep giving in whatever ways I can.

Maybe the world will never be free of "what's
wrong" but when we focus on "what's right"
too, it can only help. We see images of people
in some of the most devastating situations
laughing together. There is much evidence
that happiness heals. Yet the news is still
mostly negative, and many people still spend
more time complaining than celebrating.

I wrote *The World Goes On* at a time when
I was a bit tired of it. A pep talk from the
Soul...

Water Reflections

Being a water baby (born in July) much of my happiness comes around water. The Boise River has been a source of contentment, inspiration, healing, and joy to me. I wrote this reflection, and the following poems, after one of many days of walking along our well-loved Greenbelt, the path which travels beside the river, through and even beyond the edges of our city.

I celebrate this river, and all the magnificent bodies of water that have nourished my life.

* * *

I've never met a river I didn't like. This one, I love...the way it flows through the city, giving life to everything it touches. Giving life to the City of Trees.

If this river could talk, think of the amazing stories she would tell. Stories of a city born from nothing more than the beauty of her shores and the sustenance of her waters. Stories of passages across and along the edges of her wandering form.

Stories of early settlers, pioneers, crossing a barren desert to arrive among the hills their ancestors now call home...tales of early struggle and of families torn apart by the journey...times of celebration when people found their place within a new land.

Think of the millions of stories this river could tell about this Gem of a state that is graced with some of the most beautiful and diverse land in the country. This river is the lifeblood of the area: home to fish and water-fowl, eagles and beavers, insects and more.

Parks were born and still live along the river's shores, an intricate system of places for us to enjoy the beauty of her waters. Life stories are created here every single day.

Just think of the secrets this River could tell...

Water Travels

Listen
to the water
as it rushes by.

It flows freely,
laughing
along the way.

Beds of multi-colored
rocks, smoothed
by the river's harsh persistence.

Humbled, they arise
to their pure magnificence—
ripples of shimmering light.

A leaf journeys
on its way to the ocean; the
wind caresses my soul.

Birds ripple. Water laughs.
My heart sings
with the fullness of today.

A journey

in the space of a moment.

a celebration

49

A Cup of River

Finding the flow
of my life, as I listen
to the call of my Soul
is like
trying to capture
a fluid, raging River
into a tiny cup.

Words & actions,
no matter
how beautiful, only diminish
who I am—a futile attempt
to contain
this moving River of Life
in a moment.

Remember: the container,
no matter
how large or small,
is only a vessel.

If you hold it
too tight, it will break—
Release it!

Why seek to transform
a rushing waterfall
into a silent pool?

Become the pool
within the raging torrent
instead.

This vessel, your life,
is meant to simply
overflow.

Let your cup
dissolve: Merge
with this magnificent
River of God.

Why seek to transform
a rushing waterfall
into a silent pool?

Become the pool
within the raging torrent
instead.

Water Moments

If this River could talk,
what would she say?

Would she speak
of the ages of power
that formed this current body of life…

of rocky shores, crystal pools, and
soft sands that have eroded
time and memory?

Would she laugh
for the millions of creatures
who gain life
from her very existence?

If this River could talk,
would she tell stories
of other times;
of people who have touched her,
traveled her, shared secrets
that left her searching,
aching for more?

Would the words cascade from her lips
like the water that pours through
every minute change
of horizon she travels?

Or would her words
simply sing
a waltzing melody
into my heart
as she streams
quietly by?

Surely, if this River could talk, she
would speak
of this endless moment,

This Eternal Moment
that is opening a River in me...
as I fall into the deep
liquid pool
of her eyes.

a celebration

Water purifies.

Water cleanses.

Drip. Drip. Drip.

The water pours through

the hidden crevices

of my mind,

flushing,

emptying me of all

I thought I knew

until I am

a clear pool

once more.

Intimacy & Belonging

Let me be your ocean, washing

your debris away; freeing

what is holding you.

Be my ocean, too.

I drink you in, fall into

the depths of your waters.

You belong in me.

When I first heard the words, "you belong
in me," it was as if a symphony had just
erupted inside my chest. I knew, simply and
completely, what it was to know God through
another.

I may have experienced this connection
a hundred or thousand times before, but
somehow this simple phrase struck a chord
in my heart that until that moment had
not been played. Even now, these words
create a different kind of music in me. A
remembering: I know you…you are part of
me…I welcome you home.

You belong in me. I belong in you. We belong
not *to* one another, but we are *of* one another.
As we open to this level of deep belonging,
we indeed become oceans for one another,
washing away what locks us inside, keeps us
separate.

I dedicate this section to the many rich
friendships that have formed me, and to the
deep place of communion I have found from
this intricate dance we call relationship.

The bread of angels

A single gaze can pierce the veil.
A single Word, open a Gate.

I don't remember much, dancing
for God...singing my prayers,
but this I remember: the way your eyes
beheld me as beloved Friend;

the gentle caress of hand
embracing hand, fingers
grazing cheek, exquisite touch
of heart greeting heart.

"The bread of angels
is to touch the face of God."

One gaze. One word. One touch.
I fall.

Let this ocean carry us Home.

Reflection

I wrote this poem after a particularly
powerful connection during a Dances of
Universal Peace event at Lava hotsprings.
I remember the moment and the deep
connection that came while dancing around
the circle, peering into eyes, gently touching
the face of each beloved. As I allowed the
movement, the music, the tender caress to
embrace my heart, I felt an ocean of Love
that still sings in me.

We are portals for one another...pathways
that lead to the divinity that is available
within each moment. When we greet one
another in this way, as if we are meeting
another version of God, it doesn't take much
to fall more deeply into Love.

Imagine a world filled with nourishment of
this nature.

It's already here. Just keep opening.

Open Me

Open me, dear friend.

Read me as your favorite book.
Devour my silence
as words on a page; know me
as a story being told,
a song being sung,
a watercolor picture
erupting beneath
an Artist's brush.

Let our colors melt together
until an entirely new
One
is born.

Let our colors
melt together until

a new One
is born.

Let the sound of silence

move through...

opening a space inside.

silent grace

Background Music

Let me be
your background music.
Let me lull you
into peace, play
through you
like a wandering
stream.

The music I sing
may not be heard, unless
you quiet
your own song
for a few endless notes.

Let the sound of silence
move through us
to open
a space inside;

and here, blending
separate notes,
we shall ease each other
into perfect harmony.

Calm Deep Water Lake
in celebration of becoming 50

God is in my eyes today
reflecting all I see
in this still blue lake of sky.

The sun rises & sets
in a single perfect moment,
poetic drops
fall lightly through my mind,

Evaporating almost as quickly
and completely as the wisps of cloud
that were just here. Almost.

Instead the drops turn to music:
misty fragments of friendship & love
that sing me, each day,
more fully into being.

Memories woven deep—life and death,
an intricate dance, forever forming
this rich tapestry that becomes my life.

Molly wrote of me: calm deep water lake.
I fall in. And there you are too.

Together may we drown
in this infinite pool
of Love.

photo by Ruth Moorhead

Intimacy

Perhaps you think you know
my favorite colors
by the clothes I wear,
but my heart would tell you
my favorite color is a rainbow,
or the sun-glow
that rises from the radiant ocean
as mist transforms
the dying light
of day.

Perhaps you know that I love
to dance and sing and laugh and cry,
but can you ever know
how my heart grows
when I do. . .or how easily
my heart breaks
when you won't look
inside of me?

I tell you I love you
and you might know I am sincere,
and still you won't feel the pain I feel
when you don't believe me...

or when you don't love yourself
enough.

I was never good at small talk,
though I've learned to use it
to fill up space; and maybe you
have noticed
the space inside of me
that hasn't yet learned to trust;
the space that still feels empty

when I forget
that I am you
and you are me
and the only path to intimacy
is to open the door
we somehow built
between
the two of us.

The only path

to intimacy

is to open the door…

dance of intimacy by Sor'a

Liquid Fire

You might know me
as a calm lake, or a
gently flowing stream;

but really, I am
a pulsing waterfall
with power
beyond words.

Meet me here,
where raw energy
radiates
liquid fire.

Fall with me
into the depths
we *all* yearn for:

deep pool of Union,
ecstatic Love.

Communion

No words can express
the devotion I feel inside;
the pure adoration
that swells before me.

My heart IS this ocean,
and I am soaring
as a bird
against the sun-beamed sky.

We are not the same, you and I,
yet no different.

Watching the ocean crest & break
against a rocky shore, we sigh
in ecstatic gratitude
as this picture paints before us.

If you want the truth,
look for it in my eyes—
tears streaming like rain
on the window pane.

If you would know my joy,
my love, my desire,
feel it in the sound of my heart
as it beats into yours
in silent
communion.

Reflection

We are not the same, you and I, yet no different...

So intricate, this dance of belonging. We
come into this life dependent on others, then
spend much of our lives striving to be unique,
fighting for independence from our parents,
our families...rebelling against authority or
being overcome by it. How easy to lose our
true identity by trying to belong!

The relationship poems I chose to include
in this book are mostly a testimony to the
times I felt deeply met, though a few speak to
a missed intimacy and a desire to be known
beneath the surface where I sometimes don't
even quite know myself...a gift to show me
who I Am beyond the form, where we are all
connected.

There are still times I focus more on the
differences, but it's becoming impossible to
miss the ways we are connected. Everywhere
I turn, there is proof of interdependence;
and I continue to be amazed and delighted
by the way our unique gifts weave into such a
beautifully complete whole.

The next poem was written after my first women's circle where I experienced the wholeness that comes from honoring each unique voice. This was the first time I truly learned what it is to hold space, to listen one another into fullness as each voice is welcomed and encouraged to speak what feels most true in the moment.

Sacred Circle has become an essential part of my life, and every time I experience the richness of connecting in this extremely honoring way, I am grateful. This form of relating has taught me the art of listening well to another, while it has also helped me know myself more completely and be open to what God wants to speak through me.

As I write this reflection, I am realizing that this way of deepening connection with others through sacred circle is a kind of poetry. It speaks to what is essential, going beneath the surface of normal conversation. It peels away the layers to uncover hidden treasure, and often what comes is a surprise.

I celebrate Circles everywhere, along with the unfolding poetry of this precious life.

Circle

The music begins.
Notes play across this sacred space,
connecting separate lives.

Hesitantly at first, then
with rising tempo,
the voices ebb and flow:
currents of Truth
sent forth from the Soul.

Your heart beats in me
as I become lost
in your lucid eyes;
a crescendo of emotion
resolves with a sigh.

Every note is pure and strong,
even those sung
through a chord of fear.

Every note is beautiful,
sent forth to seek a safe home,
welcome at last.

And as the breath of life
calls forth this rendering so deep,
asking us to remember
all we had forgotten,

the time comes a last
to let go.

Hearts unite, and
the Circle is complete.

a celebration

77

Gratitude List

Rainbow-trimmed Clouds, the
song of birds outside
my window,
a yellow rose that stays
beautifully on my
dashboard
where I laid it one
summer day…

friendships that bubble up
inside me when I'm sad,
laughter…sighs…
tears that fall when
least expected,
and the golden glow of evening
as the sun takes
its final bow.

The hug of kids, dogs,
and teddy bears…
sitting quietly with a sun-yellow bird
on my shoulder,
her peep waking me
when I forget she's there;

the smell of vanilla
and peaches,
the sound of fish
swimming,
the color of the seasons
as they pass by,

and the colors that grow
inside of me
as I awake
to the possibilities
of each new day.

Giving Thanks

It's the little things
that melt my heart the most—

an unexpected gift, baby laughter,
a well-timed glance outside
to see the sun casting
glittering diamonds
upon my favorite tree,

the sound of your smile
and it whispers my name
across a crowded room.

I know you'll understand then
when I try to speak
the enormity of this Great fullness
that washes me now

and all I find
is silence.

End Note

Thank you is just a beginning, opening the door to a gratitude that grows deeper with time. Thank you for allowing these words to be shared, and for the Love they come from to be offered into your world.

I celebrate today, this new moment that is rising as I write these words, and the one that is before you now as you read them. I celebrate the blessings that are always here.

With Great Fullness,

Sor'a

a celebration

silent grace

May you find Grace
in the simple moments
and give yourself generously
to each new day.

www.ingramcontent.com/pod-product-compliance
Lightning Source LLC
Chambersburg PA
CBHW041531090426
42738CB00036B/112